DOLPHINS AND PORPOISES

BY MARIE PEARSON

The Child's World®
childsworld.com

Published by The Child's World®
1980 Lookout Drive • Mankato, MN 56003-1705
800-599-READ • www.childsworld.com

Photographs ©: iStockphoto, cover (dolphin), 2, 10, 11, 20, 24 (dolphin); Koichi Nakamura/ The Yomiuri Shimbun/AP Images, cover (porpoise), 3, 16, 21, 24 (porpoise); Michal Sen/Shutterstock Images, 5; Willyam Bradberry/Shutterstock Images, 6; Joost van Uffelen/Shutterstock Images, 9; David Hoffmann Photography/Shutterstock Images, 13; Shutterstock Images, 14, 17; Pavaphon Supanantananont/ Shutterstock Images, 19

ISBN 9781503835894
LCCN 2019943061

Printed in the United States of America

ABOUT THE AUTHOR

Marie Pearson is a children's book author and editor. She especially loves learning about animals and nature.

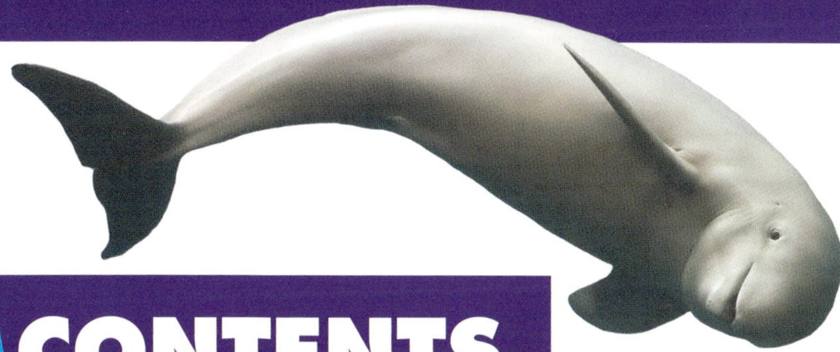

TABLE OF CONTENTS

CHAPTER

1

Mammals with Fins

A group of mammals swims under the ocean surface. Each animal has a **blowhole** on the back of its head. There is one fin on each side of its body. A **dorsal fin** pokes above the water's surface. A tail fin pushes the animal through the water. Is it a dolphin or porpoise? What's the difference?

Sea mammals such as dolphins come up to the surface to breathe air through their blowholes.

Dolphins leap out of the water to hunt or to find other dolphins. Sometimes they jump just for fun.

CHAPTER

2

Dolphins

Many dolphins are gray. Their dorsal fins are curved. Their bodies are long and **lean**. This shape helps them swim fast. They often have long **snouts**. Their teeth are cone-shaped.

There are 32 **species** of dolphin. Most live in salt water. A few live in fresh water. Dolphins often spend time near the surface of the water. They swim next to boats or leap out of the water. They eat fish and other small **aquatic** animals.

Different types of dolphins live all over the world. The Atlantic spotted dolphin is named after its home in the Atlantic Ocean.

Dolphins use their blowholes to make sounds. They use the sounds to talk with each other. Humans can hear their clicks and whistles. Dolphins also use **echolocation**. The dolphin makes sounds. The sounds hit an object and bounce back to the dolphin as an echo.

Dolphin clicks and whistles can be heard by humans.

Dolphins use the echoes to tell where objects are. Humans cannot hear these sounds.

CHAPTER

3

Porpoises

Many porpoises are gray. Their dorsal fins are shaped like triangles. Some do not have a dorsal fin at all. Their bodies are a bit **stocky**. They are smaller than dolphins. But porpoises are still fast. They have short snouts. Their teeth are flat and wide.

Dall's porpoises are black and white. Some people think they look like orcas.

Different types of porpoises can be found all over the world.

There are seven species of porpoise. Most live in salt water. Only one lives in fresh water. Porpoises usually only come to the surface to breathe. Fish are a common food for porpoises. Other aquatic animals are also **prey**.

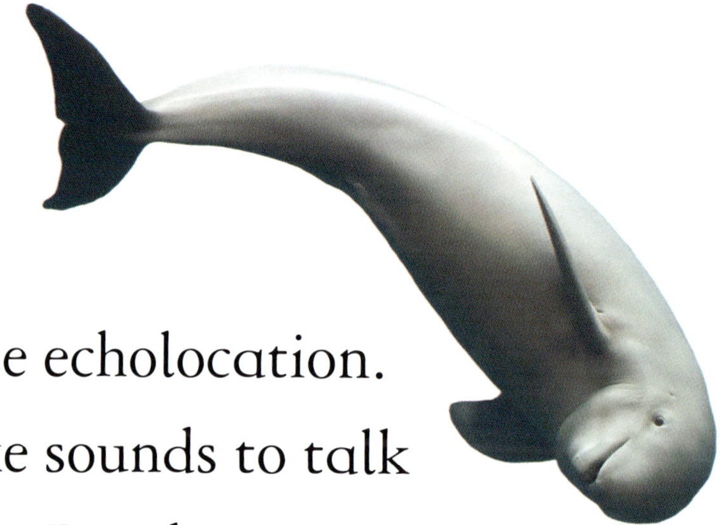

Porpoises use echolocation. They also make sounds to talk with each other. People cannot hear the sounds they make.

Porpoises rarely leap out of the water, unlike dolphins.

CHAPTER 4

What's the Difference?

Dolphins and porpoises are different in many ways. Dolphins have curved dorsal fins. Porpoises have dorsal fins shaped like triangles—or none at all. Dolphins are longer and leaner. Porpoises are shorter and stockier.

Most dolphins have longer snouts than porpoises. People can hear some of the sounds that dolphins make. People cannot hear the sounds porpoises make.

Dolphins and porpoises are both very smart. And they are both beautiful!

DOLPHINS

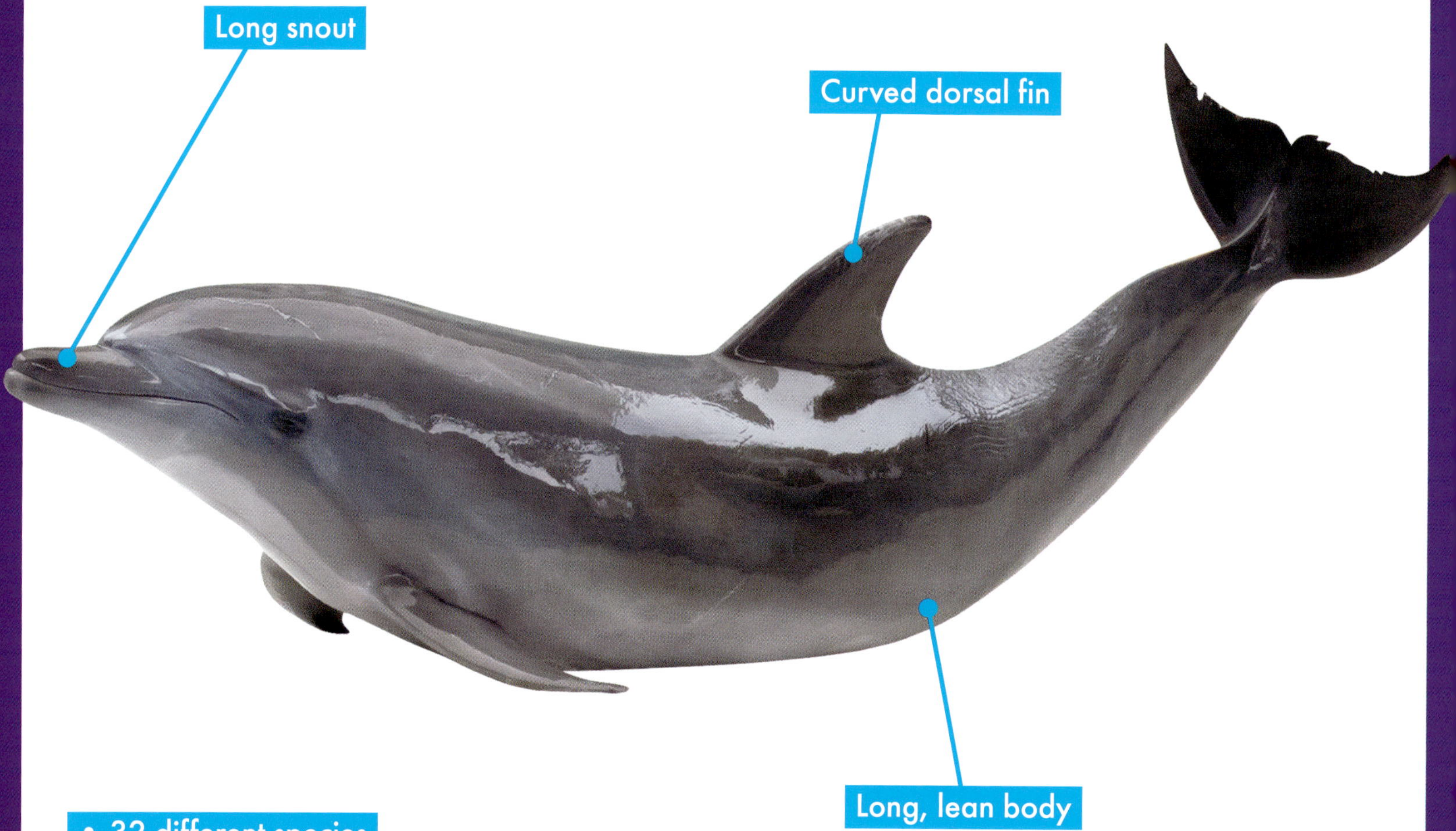

- 32 different species
- Make sounds that humans can hear
- Different species can be found in fresh water or salt water

PORPOISES

- Seven different species
- Do not make sounds humans can hear
- Only one species lives in fresh water

GLOSSARY

aquatic (uh-KWAH-tik) Something that is aquatic lives in the water. Dolphins and porpoises eat aquatic animals.

blowhole (BLOH-hole) A blowhole is a hole on the top of some marine mammals' heads through which they breathe air. A dolphin breathes through a blowhole.

dorsal fin (DOR-suhl FIN) A dorsal fin is a fin that sticks up from an animal's back. A porpoise's dorsal fin is usually triangular if it has one at all.

echolocation (ek-koh-loh-KAY-shun) Echolocation is the process of sending out sounds and sensing the way they bounce back off objects to understand how far away they are. Dolphins and porpoises use echolocation.

lean (LEEN) Something that is lean is thin. Dolphins have lean bodies.

prey (PRAY) Prey are animals that are eaten by other animals. Fish are prey for dolphins.

snouts (SNOWTS) Snouts are animals' noses. Dolphins have long snouts.

species (SPEE-sheez) A species is a group of animals that are similar and can have offspring together. There are many species of dolphins and porpoises.

stocky (STAH-kee) Something that is stocky is thick. Porpoises are stocky.

TO LEARN MORE

IN THE LIBRARY

Evans, Shira. *Dive, Dolphin!* Washington, DC: National Geographic, 2016.

Laughlin, Kara L. *Dolphins*. Mankato, MN: The Child's World, 2017.

Ryndak, Rob. *Dolphin or Porpoise?* New York, NY: Gareth Stevens Publishing, 2016.

ON THE WEB

Visit our website for links about dolphins and porpoises:
childsworld.com/links

Note to Parents, Teachers, and Librarians: We routinely verify our Web links to make sure they are safe and active sites. So encourage your readers to check them out!

ACTIVITY

Draw a picture of a dolphin and a porpoise. Your picture should clearly show the differences between the dolphin and the porpoise. Look at pages 20 and 21 for help.

INDEX

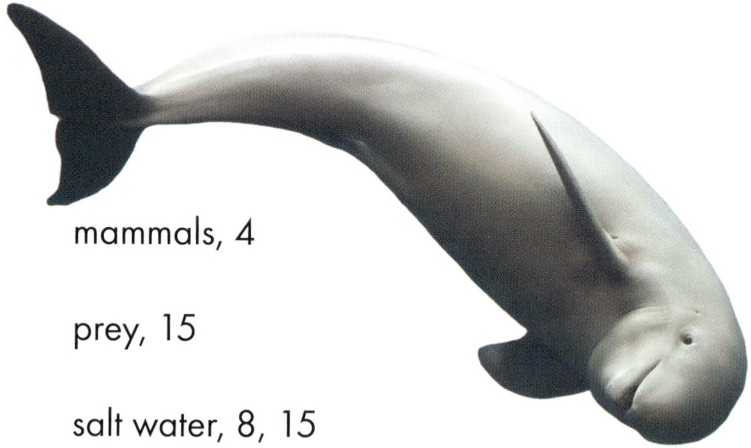